Little Book of
WOOL AND SILK
EMBROIDERY
Jenny Bradford

SALLY MILNER PUBLISHING
(MILNER CRAFT SERIES)

Introduction

In keeping with the size of the book, the examples shown are worked in fine threads. The designs can be worked on a larger scale by substituting heavier threads and enlarging the size of the pattern, making them suitable for clothing items for baby, blankets, cushions, pictures and other decorative projects.

JENNY BRADFORD, 1999.

First published in 1999 by
Sally Milner Publishing Pty Ltd
1423 Burra Road
Burra Creek 2620
New South Wales
Australia

© Jenny & Don Bradford, 1999

Design by Anna Warren, Warren Ventures, Sydney
Photography by John Tucker
Printed and bound in China

National Library of Australia
Cataloguing-in-Publication data

    Bradford, Jenny, 1936-
    Little book of wool and silk embroidery.

    Includes index.
    ISBN 1 86351 228 4.

    1. Embroidery - Patterns. 2. Silk ribbon embroidery. I.
    Title. (Series : Milner craft series)

    746.44

$\mathcal{B}$asic $\mathcal{R}$equirements

FABRICS

Wool blanketing is a popular choice for baby blankets, knee rugs etc. and is available in various weights. Thick blanketing will require the use of heavier threads (p. 5).

Medium weight brushed flannel has a firm weave that supports the stitching well and is suitable for all types of thread. It has been used for some of the samples illustrated.

Doctors flannel is a lightweight fabric ideal for delicate threads. This has also been used for some of the samples illustrated.

Other options for this type of embroidery are Afghan fabric, a synthetic fabric available from some craft outlets and wool or wool mixture dressmaking fabrics that can be utilised for cot covers etc.

Hand or machine knitted items and cotton fleece garments are also suitable for this type of decoration.

NEEDLES

Use crewel, chenille and tapestry needles suitable for the thickness of threads chosen (p. 5).

HOOPS

These are more necessary when working on fine fabrics. As a basic rule, you need a hoop if the stitching puckers the fabric without one!

STABILIZING

Stretch fabrics, or fine fabrics where heavy stitching is used, may need stabilizing for best results.

Back the design area with a piece of fine voile, silk organza or similar fabric to stabilize. Work through both layers then, if necessary, trim the backing fabric away around the design area.

TO TRANSFER A DESIGN

Wool fabric is often difficult to mark and I find the following method works well.

Draw the required outline, such as a heart, on a sheet of paper, position on the back of the fabric, then, using thread to match the fabric, machine stitch around the outline and tear away the paper. To use this method without a sewing machine, copy on to tissue paper and tack the outline with small tacking stitches before tearing away the paper carefully. Remember that the design on the right side of the fabric will be the reverse of the design drawn on the paper. When backing the fabric with voile, trace the design directly onto the voile with a fine line waterproof marker pen then position the backing fabric and use tacking stitches to mark key elements of the design to the right side of the fabric. As the design will be visible through the voile it can be placed facing the fabric so that the design is not reversed.

IDEAS FOR USING THE DESIGNS

Make a sampler quilt or cot cover by working the designs on squares of fabric, or divide a larger piece into squares with lace, ribbon or fabric strips and embroider alternate squares with your favourite designs.

Use a design to decorate a plain jumper; beads can be added as additional embellishment (see heart design p.10).

Scatter single flowers or tiny sprays over garments, baby wear etc.

THREADS

The range of available silks and wools is growing rapidly, particularly in the area of hand dyed threads, making it impossible to list a truly comprehensive range.

I suggest you experiment with any silk and wool available, bearing in mind that fabric with a fluffy pile (e.g. thick blanketing) will require thicker threads to stand out as fine threads will sink into the pile and get lost.

On pages 6 & 7 I have grouped threads according to thickness.

Threads listed in each grouping are generally interchangeable and, in many cases, silk can be substituted for wool and vice versa.

To work any design on a larger scale select thicker threads for the project and enlarge the design accordingly.

Remember there are no set rules, the most important thing is that the results please you.

HELPFUL HINTS FOR WORKING THE DESIGNS

• Design details are always listed in order of working.
• In the diagrams each new step in depicted by solid lines with previous steps shown in dotted lines.
• Except where stated, colour plates show actual size of original designs. Photocopy the plates, enlarging where necessary, to provide a pattern to transfer to your fabric.

Thread Sampler

CHART OF THREADS

	SILK	WOOL
Fine Equivalent to 1-2 strands of DMC stranded cotton	a YLI stranded b Caron Waterlilies stranded c Madeira stranded d Au Ver a Soie stranded e Kacoonda fine f Gumnut Stars g Au Ver a Soie — Goblins high sheen h Kanagawa Silk Stitch high sheen	a Kacoonda fine b Appletons crewel c Needle Necessities overdyed d DMC e Cascade Yarns 1 ply f Fancyworks fine g Gumnut Daisies
Medium Equivalent to 3-4 strands of cotton	i Kacoonda high twist j Colour Streams Ophir high sheen	h Kacoonda mohair i NZ Royal Stitch j Torokina k Mogear Mohair l NZ Strand
Thick Equivalent to 4-6 strands of cotton	k Gumnut Buds Jewels l Kacoonda thick m Colour Streams Exotic high sheen n Au Ver a Soie Perle high sheen o Kanagawa K1000 buttonhole twist high sheen	m Gumnut Blossoms n Fancyworks thick o Kacoonda Medium p Cascade Yarns 2 ply q Kaleidocolours

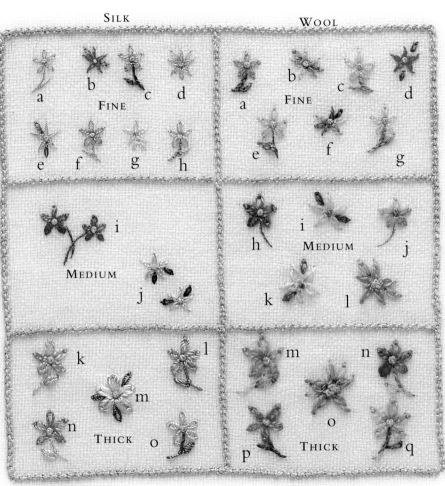

FINE

a   b   c   d

FINE

a   b   c   d

e   f   g   h

e   f   g

MEDIUM

i

j

MEDIUM

h   i   j

k   l

THICK

k   l   m   n   o

THICK

m   n   o   p   q

$\mathscr{M}$AUVE GARLAND

WOOLS
Gumnut Daisies 644 light
*   khaki green*
Gumnut Daisies 295 pale lavender

SILKS
Kacoonda fine 9 pink
Gumnut Stars 991 ecru, 745 mid
*   gold, 628 dark green*
Colour Streams Ophir 1 high sheen
*   wisteria, pale mauve/blue*
Kanagawa Silk Stitch high sheen
*   170 dark pink*

Work feather stitch circle in 644 wool, adding side stems.

Work petals for 5-petal flowers, and buds, in 295 wool, using straight stitch (a, b, c).

Highlight in high sheen silk 1 by working fly stitch from tips of adjacent petal into flower (d). Work a straight stitch up the centre of each petal (e). Work a colonial knot at centre in silk 745. Complete buds with fly stitch in silk 628.

Pink 4-petal flowers are worked as detailed in diagrams (3 stitches only for each petal) using 9 wool. Highlight with a silk 170 cross stitch over the centre of flower (f), finishing centre with a colonial knot in 745.

Work white buds in silk 991 completing with fly stitch in 628.

Finally add fly stitch leaves in 644 wool (see p. 14).

a   b   c

start 5 petal
flowers with 3
marker petals

add last 2
petals in
large spaces

d

e

f

ℬEADED HEART

WOOLS
Gumnut Daisies 193 light wine, 195 wine

SILKS
Gumnut Stars 387 mid cornflower blue, 587 mid fern green, 745 mid gold
Colour Streams Ophir high sheen 7 fuchsia, soft crimson through to purple

The flowers used in this design are worked as detailed on p.8.

Complete outline using 587 silk, whipped chain stitch (2 strands) and feather stitching (1 strand).

Work 5-petal flowers in 193 wool and highlight in 7 silk.

Add blue 4-petal flowers and buds in 387 silk, then pink 4-petal flowers and buds in 193 wool.

Fill flower centres with a colonial knot in silk 745 (3 strands for large flowers).

Finish with lazy daisy leaves in silk 587 then add pearls or colonial knots.

This design is suitable for a garment. If using it on a baby blanket, work colonial knots in 2 or 4 mm silk ribbon or heavy silk thread such as Lame Silk by Cascade Yarns to replace the pearls.

Reproduced at 90% of original

Wools

*Gumnut Blossoms 843 light coral,
    855 mid salmon*
*Gumnut Daisies 405 light aqua, 644
    light khaki green, 855 mid salmon*

Silks

*Gumnut Stars 746 gold,
    949 dark tan*
*Colour Streams Ophir high sheen
    8 apricot blush, pastel yellow
    through to apricot*

All flowers, buds and leaves are worked in uneven lazy daisy (p.44).

Mark an oval for the centre of the daisies; size will depend on thickness of thread and size of finished flower. Work in wool 855 and 843 for large daisies (a) and thinner wool 855 & 405 for half daisies and medium daisies (b).

Work tiny 5-petal flowers in silk 8 (c).

Complete centres of flowers with colonial knots in 746 and 949 silk using 1 strand for small flowers and 2 strands for large flowers.

Complete with uneven lazy daisy stitch leaves in 644 wool. Highlight some with contrast silk straight stitch down centre.

a

b

c

work 4
marker
petals

fill in spaces
with as many
petals as will fit

work 3
marker
petals

fill in large
gaps with 2
petals

Reproduced at
80% of original

$\mathcal{D}$AISY CHAIN

WOOLS
Gumnut Daisies 745 mid gold,
746 gold

SILKS
Gumnut Stars 587 mid fern green,
969 dark brown

Transfer design and mark stem positions as detailed.
Work outline and stems in whipped chain using a single
strand of 587 silk.

Work daisies and half daisies as described on p.12
using 745 and 746 wool.

Fill daisy centres with colonial knots in 969 silk.

Work fly stitch leaves with one strand of 587 silk on
stems of single daisies.

This corner design can be reversed and repeated to cre-
ate a square.

*Reproduced at
90% of original*

$\mathcal{W}$INDBLOWN FLOWERS

WOOLS
Gumnut Daisies 991 ecru

SILKS
Gumnut Stars 991 ecru, 587 mid
fern green, 823 light bright coral
Colour Streams Ophir high sheen
1 wisteria, pale mauve/blue,
3 musk rose, mid pink/mauve

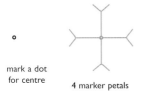

mark a dot
for centre

4 marker petals

fill in with as
many stitches
as required

Mark placement for the larger flowers. The smaller flowers can be scattered at random.

Work white flowers first in extended fly stitch. Work first circle of petals in wool 991. Add a second circle of petals in silk 991. 'Blown' petals are worked using wool and silk 991.

Scatter smaller flowers over the area, working only 1 row of petals in silks 1, 3 and 823.

Add stems in whipped chain or stem stitch using 587 silk.

*Reproduced at
90% of original*

ℋORSESHOE OF FLOWERS

WOOLS

Gumnut Daisies 386 cornflower blue,
*   644 light khaki green, 947 tan*
Needle Necessities 62 lemon

SILKS

Gumnut Stars 297 lavender, 387 mid
*   cornflower blue, 708 butter yellow*
Colour streams Ophir high sheen
*   4 straw, strong yellow/orange/lime*

Use a hoop for this
project if possible.

 Work large yellow
flower in 62 wool
using pistil stitch.
Work a long stitch up
the centre of the petal then fill in, working on each side alternately.

 Add pistil or straight stitch highlights around centre in silk 4, then fill centre with colonial knots in 947 wool.

 Work stem stitch stems in 644 wool.

 Add blue flowers, working step 1 in 386 wool, step 2 in 387 silk.

 Add fan flowers, working step 1 in 62 wool, step 2 in 708 silk.

 Work lilacs in colonial knots using 297 silk, then scatter colonial knots in 4 silk.

 Finally add fly stitch leaves in 644 wool (see p. 14).

blue flowers and fan-shaped buds

lilac — colonial knots

step 1   step 2

*F*LORAL SWAG

WOOLS
*DMC 8405 olive green,
8816 deep pink*

SILKS
*Gumnut Stars 387 mid cornflower
blue, 709 mid yellow
Kanagawa Silk stitch high sheen
170 deep pink*

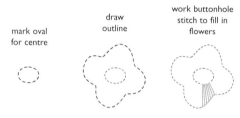

mark oval for centre

draw outline

work buttonhole stitch to fill in flowers

Work large pink flowers in buttonhole stitch in 8816 wool. Matching silk can be used to highlight around centre as in pistil stitch flowers on previous page.

Fill in centre with colonial knots using 709.

Work leaves in buttonhole stitch in wool 8405. Add side stems in stem stitch and same thread.

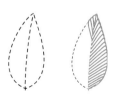

draw leaf shape with centre vein

Add blue buds in silk 387. 7 or 8 buttonhole stitches are worked into a central point at the base of the bud.

Work small pink flowers in buttonhole stitch in 8816 wool and 170 silk working into the same hole in the centre each time.

Finally add lazy daisy leaves in wool 8405.

*Reproduced at
90% of original*

$\mathcal{D}$AISY SWAG

WOOLS

Gumnut Daisies 405 light aqua,
*   947 tan*
DMC 8405 olive green
Kacoonda Fine 6F tropical coral
Cascade Yarns 1 ply 47 variegated green

SILKS

Gumnut Stars 587 mid fern green,
*   709 mid yellow, 991 ecru*
Kacoonda High Twist 6F tropical coral
*   & 8B shaded dark green, 103*
*   antique gold*

All flowers, buds, leaves and butterfly are worked in lazy daisy stitch.

Large daisies are worked first with 2 layers of petals, 1 in wool 6F and 1 in silk 6F. Anchor second row between petals of first row.

Fill the centre with colonial knots in wool 947.

Using wool 47, work stems in feather stitch and add leaves starting at leaf tip and anchoring at the base.

Work blue daisies next in wool 405. Mark centre with a dot. Work marker petals as for large daisies and add 1 petal between marker petals. Add silk highlights in 8B with a straight stitch up the centre of the petals. Complete colonial knot centres in 709. Work stems of blue daisies in wool 8405 in large feather stitch.

Buds are worked in silk 991 and 587. Work 1 lazy daisy stitch then add a fly stitch around the base in the same colour. Finish with straight stitch and fly stitch in green.

Complete tiny daisies with 4 marker petals only in wool 6F and 947 colonial knots in centre.

Butterfly wings are worked in silk 6F and 103 with a straight stitch body in silk.

Reproduced at
90% of original

$\mathscr{P}$EACH BOW

WOOLS
Fancyworks thick peach

SILKS
Gumnut Stars 587 mid fern green
Gumnut Buds 825 mid bright coral

Enlarge bow to
required size

Transfer the outline and work in
palastrina stitch in peach wool.

Stitches must be kept close to
maintain an even texture. Fill knot
in straight stitch in same thread.

Work stems in feather stitch
using 1 strand of silk 587.

Add palastrina buds in silk 825.
Bring the needle up at the tip of the
bud in line with the stem. Position the
stitch as shown in the diagram.

Complete the stitch as illustrated
(p.45) and anchor in line with the
stem.

Reproduced at
90% of original

ℋEARTS AND BUNNIES

WOOLS

Gumnut Daisies 346 mid dull blue,
  644 light khaki green, 947 tan
Appletons crewel 943 bright rose pink
Mogear Mohair 1 white

SILKS

Gumnut Stars 644 light khaki green
Kacoonda high twist 6F tropical coral
Colour Streams Ophir high sheen
  4 straw, 2 water nymphs blue

Stem stitch heart outlines in wool 644. Add side stems on large heart.

Work pink flowers and buds in wool 943. Highlight with silk 6F (see p.12 for flowers). Then work blue flowers and buds on small heart in wool 346. Highlight with silk 2. All buds are in lazy daisy stitch.

Add the blue buds on the large heart in palastrina stitch in wool 346 (see p.45).

Work all leaves in fly stitch (p.14) using wool 644 (large heart) and silk 644 (small heart).

Using wool 947 work rabbits in straight stitch following the diagrams carefully.

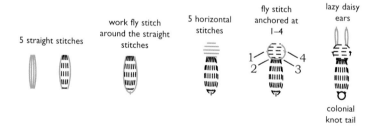

5 straight stitches

work fly stitch around the straight stitches

5 horizontal stitches

fly stitch anchored at 1–4

lazy daisy ears

colonial knot tail

Complete with colonial knot flowers in silk 4 around rabbits.

*Reproduced at
90% of original*

ℱLORAL SHEAF

WOOLS
Kacoonda medium 5 wisteria
Kacoonda fine 9b pink

SILKS
Gumnut Stars 587 mid fern green
Colour Streams Ophir high sheen
7 fuchsia, soft crimson through to
apricot

First work branches to required shape in feather stitch using silk 587.

Large flowers are worked next in wool 5. These are woven (a). Weave over and under spokes packing the rows close together so that the flower is raised up. Pass the needle to the back of the work and secure

Leaves are also woven in silk 587. Lay spokes, couching outer threads into a leaf shape. Weave as before from base to tip (b).

Next work fan flowers in wool 9 (c).

Work small star flowers in silk 7 (d).

Add lazy daisy leaves in silk 587 and finally add pearls.

make a 5 spoke
foundation

a

weave over and
under spokes

b

lay foundation

weave under
and over
spokes in rows

c

weave spokes
by backstitching
over spokes

d

Wombat

SILKS

Gumnut Stars 387 mid cornflower
  blue, 389 very dark cornflower
  blue, 587 mid fern green,
  745 mid gold, 969 dark brown

DMC stranded cotton 838
  dark brown
DMC Perle 12 301 black

This wombat is worked on homespun, cut out and applied to the fabric.

Enlarge pattern and draw onto fabric, work long and short stitch in the direction of the arrows on the pattern using 969 single strand. Work the head stitching over the stitching on the back at the neckline.

Back the design with an iron-on bonding material and cut out the wombat carefully, cutting around paws and nose markings which will be embroidered later. Position onto the fabric and iron from the back to bond lightly. Stitch in place by working over the edge in long stitches keeping them in line with the body stitching.

Work ears in fly stitch in 969 with centre in 838.

Nose and feet are 838 in straight stitch through all thicknesses. Eyes are colonial knots in black surrounded by bullion stitches in 969.

Work dry grasses in whipped chain and palastrina stitch for buds,

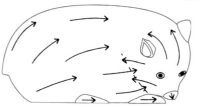

straight stitch for shorter leaves, using 745, then flowers in colonial knots and lazy daisy stitch using 387 and 389 with colonial knot centre in 745. Add grass in 587 in straight stitch. Finally work stones in colonial knots in 587 and 969.

ℛoses

WOOLS

Fancyworks Fine avocado
Cascade Yarns 2 ply 4715
  variegated pink

SILKS

Gumnut Stars 679 dark golden olive
2 mm silk ribbon 156 cream

Work stems in whipped chain in avocado wool.

Work bullion stitch roses in wool 4715 following the stitch placements shown.

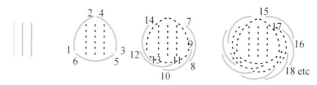

Work buds in straight stitch in wool 4715. Work 3 stitches for centre of bud (a). Add a twisted fly stitch across tip of stitches (b). Lay 4 stitches in each direction across the base (c). Lay 2 bullion stitches, 1 short, 1 long, along the edges of the stitches just worked (d).

Work straight and fly stitches around base of buds in silk 679 (d). Work fly stitch leaves in silk 679 (p.14).

Finally work bow in whipped running stitch using silk ribbon (p.47).

$\mathcal{I}$NTERLOCKING HEARTS

WOOLS
Gumnut Daisies 405 light aqua,
*   823 light bright coral*

SILKS
Gumnut Stars 647 khaki green, 709
*   yellow, 823 light bright coral, 825*
*   mid bright coral, 827 bright coral*
Colour Streams Ophir high sheen
*   9 peaches, pink through to apricot*

The shading of the hearts is created by rows of closely stitched stem stitch in graduated colours of silk. Work stem stitch outlines of hearts in 827. Work two rows in each of 823 and 825. Then work final row in 827 again.

Large leaves are worked in silk 647 in fly stitch. Mark onto fabric and then fill in. Outline leaf in stem stitch.

Work pistil stitch flower in wool 823 and fill centre with colonial knots in 9 (p. 18 blue flowers).

The forget-me-nots are worked with a colonial knot in centre in 709 silk, surrounded by 5 or 6 colonial knots in wool 405.

Reproduced at
90% of original

Rabbits

Wools

Fancyworks thick dusk
Fancyworks fine dusk
Gumnut Blossoms white or
* white mohair*

Silks

Gumnut Stars 969 dark brown
Kanagawa K1000 buttonhole twist
* high sheen 825 apricot*
Colour Streams Ophir high sheen 6
* harvest, pastel lemon, antique*
4 mm Fancyworks overdyed no. 17
* variegated green*

Outline large rabbit in whipped chain in thick dusk wool. Outline small rabbit in whipped chain fine dusk wool.

Work features in straight and stem stitch in silk 969.

Add white tails in colonial knots.

Work looped bullion stitch flowers with 25 wraps for each stitch in 825 silk.

Work colonial knots in 6 in centre of each flower.

Make neck bow for large rabbit in ribbon. Cut a short length, fold as shown and stitch in place with a straight stitch over the centre. Adjust

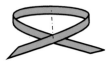

bow size then work one or two more stitches over the centre.

Place ribbon with 2 tiny loops on neckline of small rabbit before working a tiny 3 loop flower. Work centre with a colonial knot.

Teddy Bear

WOOLS
DMC 8845 dark tan, 8846 light tan

SILKS
DMC Perle 12 301 black
Colour Streams Ophir high sheen 6
   harvest, pastel lemon, antique
7 mm Kacoonda silk ribbon no. 105
   antique autumn

Outline bear using one strand each of 8845 and 8846 in whipped chain.

Stem stitch all inner design lines in single strand of darker shade.

Using single strand, seed stitch bear mixing 8845 and 8846 as illustrated.

Straight stitch muzzle and ears in 8846.

Satin stitch nose, stem stitch mouth and work colonial knots for eyes, all in black.

Fill pads with lazy daisy stitches in 6.

Work looped bullion flowers in 6 (see p.36). Fill centres with colonial knots.

Fold and stitch ribbon for bow as on p.36.

ℬASKET

WOOLS
Kacoonda 6c dusty earth

SILKS
Gumnut Jewels dark agate

Trace basket pattern onto voile then
stiffen the area with iron-on Vilene.
Position behind fabric and tack in place.
Place fabric in a hoop.

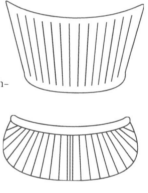

   Tack basket shape through to right
side. Outline the sides of basket 1 and the
full shape of basket 2 with tiny chain stitches in dark agate silk. Stitch vertical lines
in long stitches as indicated using dark
agate.

   Weave wool 6c over and under
threads to fill shape starting at the base
of basket 1 and the top centre of basket
2, taking care not to pull too tight.

   Finish top of both baskets and bottom of basket 1 with a row of
whipped chain in wool 6c.

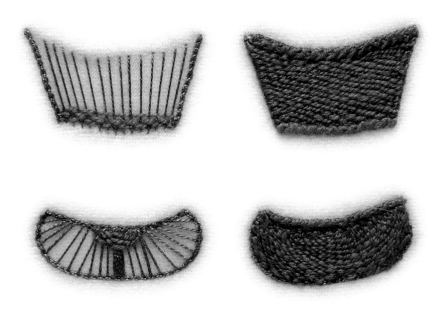

$\mathcal{S}$titch glossary

On all stitch and flower diagrams the *odd* numbers refer to the needle passing *up* through the fabric from back to front. The *even* numbers refer to the needle passing *down* through the fabric from front to back.

BULLION STITCH

Use a straw or milliner's needle if possible and keep wraps smooth and even.

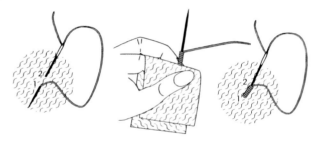

BUTTONHOLE STITCH

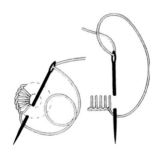

COLONIAL KNOTS

A straw or milliner's needle will give the best results. Always neaten the thread around the shaft of the needle where it pierces the fabric before passing the needle to the back of the work. Remember that the knot may pull to the back if the needle is passed up and down through the same hole.

FEATHER STITCH

This is a 'one way' stitch. Take care that all the stems point in the right direction on a design.

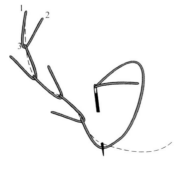

FLY STITCH AND EXTENDED FLY STITCH

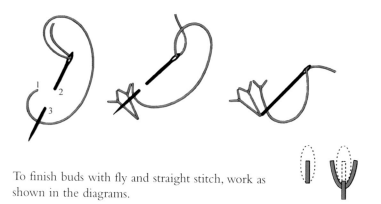

To finish buds with fly and straight stitch, work as shown in the diagrams.

LAZY DAISY AND UNEVEN LAZY DAISY

LONG AND SHORT STITCH

First row of straight stitches worked alternating long and short stitches. Subsequent rows are an even length but will appear staggered. To achieve a more natural fur effect overlap the stitches and, if desired, work some off-line stitches.

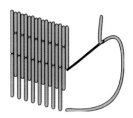

PALASTRINA STITCH

When working a line of these stitches repeat as shown in fourth diagram, keeping stitches close together to make a solid line. For single buds, anchor the stitch as shown in the fifth diagram.

PISTIL STITCH

Work in a hoop and use a milliner's needle if possible. Tighten the thread around the needle before the needle is passed to the back of the work.

SEED STITCH

Tiny straight stitches scattered over the surface in all directions.

STEM STITCH

STRAIGHT STITCH

WHIPPED CHAIN STITCH

Follow the required design line with a row of small chain stitches. Using a tapestry needle work a whip stitch into each successive chain. Different effects can be achieved by using different threads or thicknesses for each process.

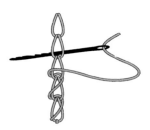

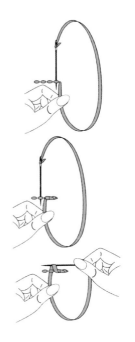

WHIPPED RUNNING STITCH

Running stitches must be slightly longer than the width of the ribbon used; stitches on the back of the work should be as small as possible. Note that when whipping, the ribbon is kept flat as the needle passes under each surface stitch twice.

WOVEN STITCHES

Use a hoop and pull foundation stitches firmly.

Flowers — Work five spokes the required size, then weave thread as shown

    A — thread over and under alternate threads.

    B — back stitch over each spoke in turn.

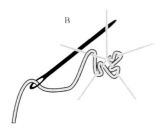

DETAILS OF COVER PIECE

ACKNOWLEDGMENTS

I would like to thank the following people for their support and generosity in supplying me with the materials for this book:

Diane Baldwin of Fancyworks, Echuca, Victoria, for wool fabric and wools;
Julie Ellis of Gumnut Yarns, Mudgee, NSW for silk and wool threads
Alan Linklater of Cotton on Creations, Epping, NSW for YLI silk threads and ribbons;
Jenny Findlay of Mogear Yarns, Jerrawa, NSW for mohair yarns;
Robyn Dowling of Cascade Yarns, Langwarrin, Victoria for wool and silk threads;
Robyn Alexander of Colour Streams, Epping, NSW for silk threads.

As always there would be no book without Sally Milner's faith in my work or the vital contribution and expertise in the drawing of diagrams, computer work and proof reading of my husband, Don.